Summerbook Readers: Book 1

Short *a* and *i* words

Angela M. Ankers

Summerbook Company
www.summerbookcompany.com

©2004 Summerbook Company.
All rights reserved. No part of this book may be reproduced without permission.

New Sight Words
a - introduced on page 4
is - introduced on page 19

ISBN 1-933055-00-6 (Book 1)
ISBN 1-933055-03-0 (3 Book Set)
Printed in the USA
Summerbook Company
www.summerbookcompany.com

cat

sat

hat

mat

bat

can

bag

rag

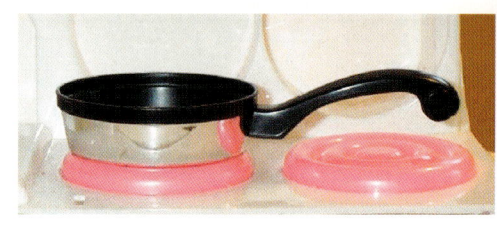
pan

van

fan

tag

cap

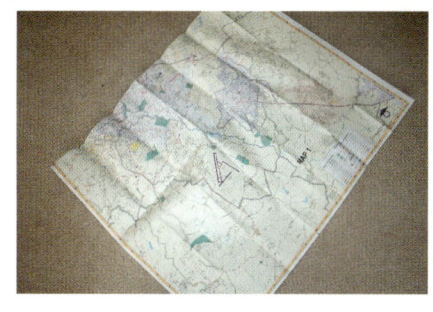
map

nap

an ax

sad Sam

Dan had Pam.

Jan had a hat.

Jan had a tag.

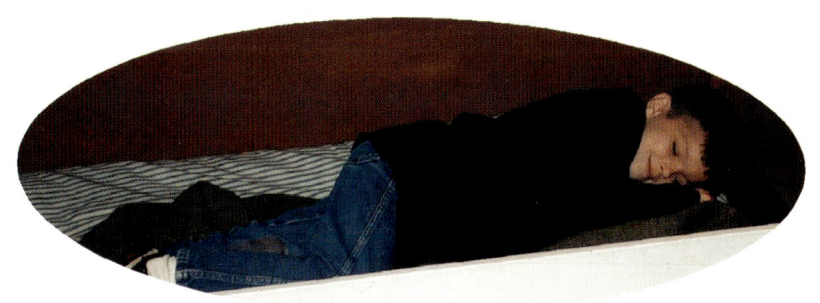

Dan can nap.

Pam had a pan.

Sam had a cap.

Dad

Sam  Dan

Dad sat.

Sam sat.

Dan sat.

Dan sat.

Dan had a hat.

Sam sat.

Sam had a hat.

Tag Sam

Dan ran.

Dan ran at Sam.

Sam ran.

Can Dan tag Sam?

Dan can tag Sam.

Sam ran.

Sam ran at Dan.

Dan ran.

Can Sam tag Dan?

Sam can tag Dan.

A Cat

A cat sat.

A fat cat sat.

A cat can nap.

A cat had a nap.

A cat can bat.

A cat can bat a tag.

Max sat.

Max sat and sat.

Max had a nap.

Max sat and had a nap.

A Fax

Dad can fax.

Dad can fax a map.

Dad can fax a man a map.

Can Dan fax?

Wax a Van

Dad had a van.

Dan had a rag.

Sam had wax and a rag.

Can Dan and Sam wax?

Dan and Sam can wax a van.

1. Al had a nap.
2. Nat had a pal.
3. A cab had gas.
4. Nan had a lap.
5. Dad had a sax.
6. Pam can act mad.
7. Can a lad wag?
8. Can Jan zap Sal?
9. Cam can ask Dad.
10. A lad had an ax.
11. Tad is a tax man.
12. A man had a lab.
13. Can Hal pat a rat?
14. Tad had a gas cap.
15. Max had a tan pad.
16. Al can tap and rap.

17. A cat can nab a rat.

18. A can had a tan tab.

19. A ram can jab a man.

20. A fat ant ran and ran.

21. Pat and Sal had a nap.

22. Al had ham and a yam.

23. Can Hal wax a tan cab?

24. Nan and Nat can ask Dad.

25. A bad lad had a mad cat.

26. Tam had an ant and a tan cat.

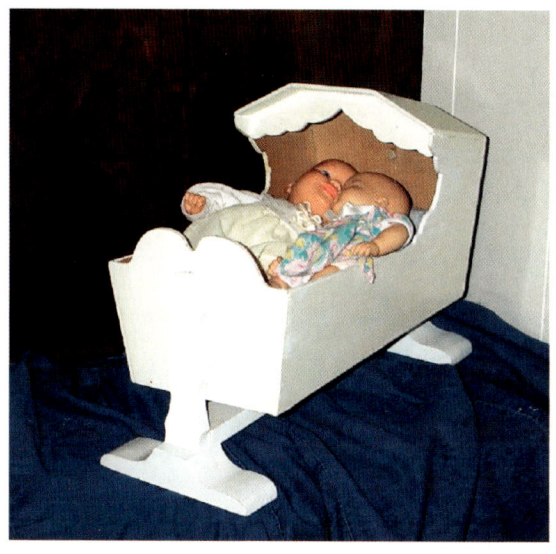

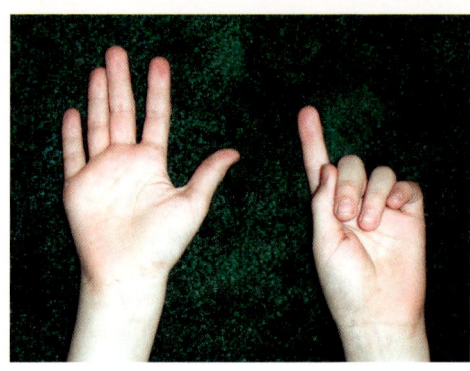

six

a bib

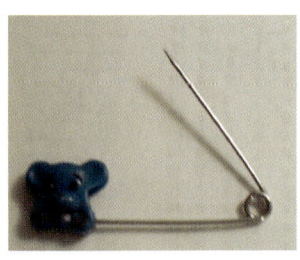
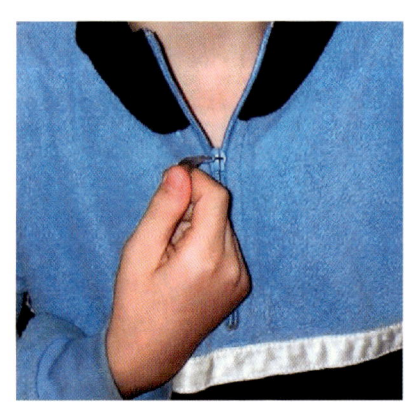

a pin   zip

dig

16

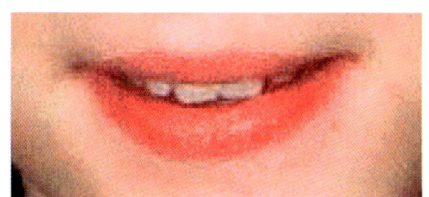

a lip

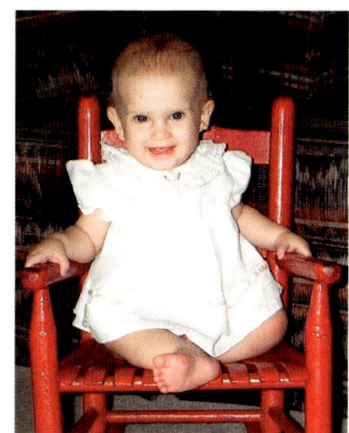

sit

win

lid

pig

Jim hid.

Tim did sip.

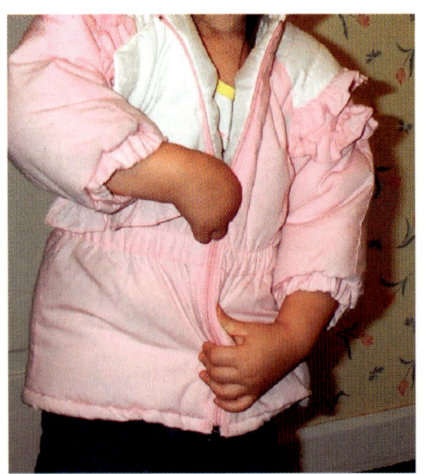

Did Liz zip?

Did Tim tip in a dip?

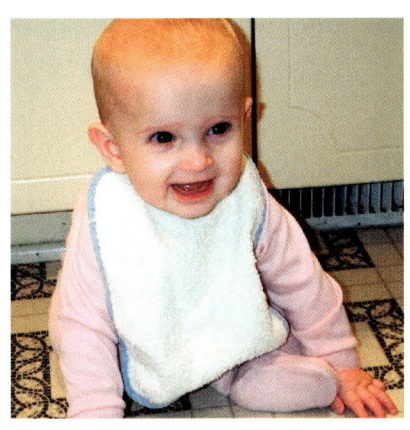

It is a big bib.

Is a pig in a bin?

A Rip in a Bib

A rip is in a bib.

Did Kim fix a rip?

Kim did fix a rip.

Kim did fix a rip in a bib.

A Pit

Did Jim dig a pit?
Jim did dig a pit.
Jim did dig a big pit.
Is Jim in a big pit?
Jim hid in a big pit.

A Tin Lid

Tim hit a lid.

It is a tin lid.

It is a big tin lid.

Tim did hit a big tin lid.

Kip

Kip is a kid.

Kip is a big kid.

Kip can nip.

Kip can nip a fig.

Kip can nip a tin lid.

Kim and a Mix

Kim had a mix.

Kim can fix it.

Kim can fix a mix.

Kim can pat it in a pan.

In a Van

Dad had a big map in a van.

Dad had gas in a van.

Pam can sit in a van.

Pam can nap in a van.

Can Dad nap in a van?

Hit It, Dan!

Can Dan hit it?
Hit it, Dan, hit it!
Dan can hit it.
Dan can tap it.
Hit it in, Dan.

Pip

Tim had Pip.
Pip is a pal.
Pip can sit in a lap.
Pip can nip a big bit.
Is Pip a big pal?

In a Bin

Jim had a bin.

Is it a big bin?

Jim hid a map in a bin.

Jim hid a pin in a bin.

Jim can sit in a bin.

A Tan Bag

Kip had a tan bag.

Kip had a big tin can.

Kip had a can in a bag.

Kip had a tin can in a tan bag.

Did Kip tip a tan bag?

Dan at Bat

Dan is at bat.

Can Dan hit it?

Hit it, Dan, hit it!

Dan did hit it!

Dan had a big hit.

Sam in a Pit

Sam and Dan can dig a pit.

It is a big pit.

Did Sam sit in a pit?

Sam sat in a pit.

Can Sam nap in a pit?

A Bad Rim

Sam had a bad rim.

Sam is sad.

Can Dad fix a bad rim?

Dad can fix it.

Dad can fix a bad rim.

Tap and Hit

Tap, tap, tap.
Sam can tap it.
Sam can hit it.
Tap it in, Sam.
Hit it, Sam, hit it!

Pam Can Act

Pam can act.

Pam can act sad.

Pam can act fat.

Pam can act big.

Did Pam act mad?

Nan Is Sad

Nan had a fan.
A fan had a rip.
It is a big rip.
Nan is sad.
Can Nan fix it?

A Lab

Dad is in a lab.

A lab had a rat and a cat.

A lab had a pan and a bin.

Dad lit gas in a lab.

Dad can mix and fix in a lab.

Pin a Tag

Sal can pin a tag.

Kim can pin a big tag.

Jan can pin a tan tag.

Liz can pin a rag tag.

Can Pam pin a tag?

Can Sam zip it?

Sam can zip it.

Can Pam zip it?

Pam can zip it.

Can Dan zip it?

Dan can zip it.

1. Did Pat win?
2. Is Max a cat?
3. Nan did ask Hal.
4. Pat can tag him.
5. A mat did sag.
6. Did a hat fit Kit?
7. A pig hit its hip.
8. Is Kit a big lad?
9. Pam and Lil can sit.
10. A mad pig did nip him.
11. A rat bit a big ham.
12. A can had jam in it.
13. Can a cat yap and yap?
14. A big man ran and ran.
15. Kim hid a pin in a bag.
16. Nan did dip it in a pan.

17. Is a tin can in a bin?
18. Max had a dab in a can.
19. Pat can nap in a big bed.
20. A lad had a fig and bit it.
21. A cat hit its lip and its rib.
22. Kim can fix a ham in a pan.
23. Did a ram in a pen hit him?
24. If Hal is a lad, can Hal wag?
25. A big, tan mat had a gap in it.
26. A tan kit had a map and a can in it.

Other Summerbook Company Products for Young Children

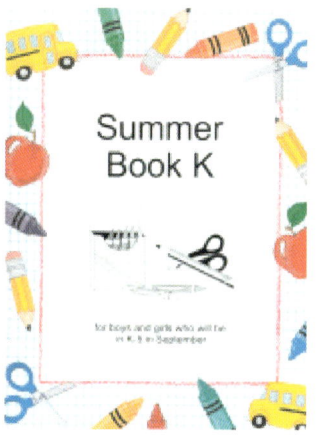

Summer Book K is for students who will be entering kindergarten (K-5) in the fall. It contains sixty pages of activities. The front of each page is for the child to do. The back of each page contains tips and suggestions for parents. The answer key is located at the back of the book and may easily be removed.

The *Summer Book K* packet includes:
- *Summer Book K*
- Magnetic upper and lower case letters
- Magnetic numbers
- Colored shapes

Topics in *Summer Book K* include:
- larger and smaller
- matching
- letter sounds
- writing letters
- colors
- right and left

Visit us on the web at www.summerbookcompany.com!

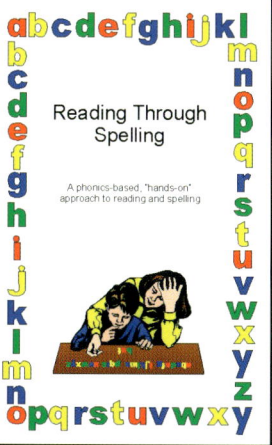

Reading Through Spelling is based upon the premise that while people can often read words that they cannot later spell, people are seldom able to spell words that they cannot read. This book is designed to help you as a parent teach your child to read by helping your child become a good speller. *Reading Through Spelling* begins with two-letter, short-vowel words. The book contains word lists and explanations of the spelling principles for other short-vowel words, consonant blends, digraphs (sh, ch, th, wh, ph) and long-vowel words. It also contains a list of the three hundred most commonly used words. Each book comes with two sets of lower-case magnetic letters.

In this alphabet all the vowels are red, and only the vowels are red. This helps young children learn that each word must have a vowel. The "b" and "d" are also different colors to help avoid confusion. The color of each lower-case letter matches the color of the upper case letter.

The letters are made of two layers. The top layer is a rubbery foam, and the bottom layer is magnetic. These letters will stick solidly without sliding or turning yet are easy to pick up and move.

These numerals offer a hands-on way to practice counting and place value, as well as simple operations.

Order these and other products on the web at
www.summerbookcompany.com.

Don't get eaten! The object of this game is to get as many dinosaurs as possible into herds of two or more. When played with simplified rules, this game is great for kindergarteners and children in the lower elementary grades. The dice are 16mm. Each game comes with six dice and directions.

Build a better train! When played by the simple rules, this fun game teaches counting and addition. The dice are 18mm. The game comes with six dice and directions.